SUMMER MATH WORKBOOK

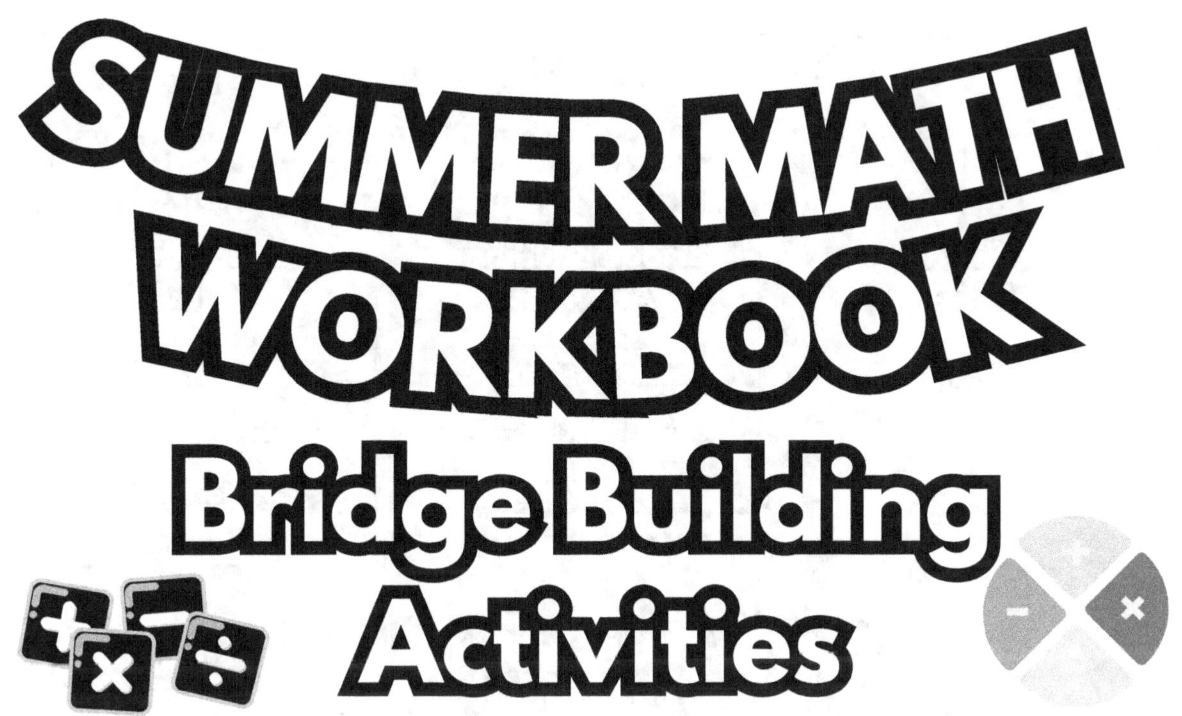

Grade
1 → 2
SUMMER MATH WORKBOOK
Bridge Building Activities
Number Sense
Addition and Subtraction
Place Value

Grade
2 → 3
SUMMER MATH WORKBOOK
Bridge Building Activities
Number Sense
Addition and Subtraction
Place Value

Grade
3 → 4
SUMMER MATH WORKBOOK
Bridge Building Activities
Number Sense
Addition and Subtraction
Place Value

Grade
4 → 5
SUMMER MATH WORKBOOK
Bridge Building Activities
Multiplication and Division
Place Value and Units
Fractions and Geometry

Grade
5 → 6
SUMMER MATH WORKBOOK
Bridge Building Activities
Multiplication and Division
Factors and Multiples
Fractions and Geometry

Grade
6 → 7
SUMMER MATH WORKBOOK
Bridge Building Activities
Arithmetic
Algebra
Geometry and Statistics

Grade
7 → 8
SUMMER MATH WORKBOOK
Bridge Building Activities
Ratio and Percentage
Algebra and Cartesian Plane
Geometry and Statistics

Grade
8 → 9
SUMMER MATH WORKBOOK
Bridge Building Activities
Ratio and Percentage
Algebra
Geometry and Graphing

Grade
9 → 10
SUMMER MATH WORKBOOK
Bridge Building Activities
Factoring and Distributing
Algebra
Geometry and Graphing

Introduction

As parents and educators, we understand the pivotal role that mathematics plays in shaping a child's academic journey and future success. Yet, the path to mathematical proficiency can often seem daunting, filled with challenges and complexities. That's where the transformative power of Summer Bridge Building Activities books comes into play, illuminating the way forward with clarity, precision, and purpose.

Summer vacation is a time for rest and relaxation, but it also presents the risk of the "summer slide," where students lose some of the academic gains they made during the school year. Summer Bridge Building Activities books are specifically designed to tackle this challenge, ensuring that your child stays academically engaged and prepared for the upcoming school year. These books provide a seamless bridge from one grade to the next, reinforcing essential skills and introducing new concepts that will give your child a head start.

Imagine your child eagerly diving into the pages of a Summer Bridge Building Activities book, greeted by clear, engaging content that demystifies complex mathematical concepts. With each turn of the pages, they embark on a journey of discovery, encountering thoughtfully curated practice questions that reinforce learning and sharpen problem-solving skills. As they unveil the answers to those questions, a sense of accomplishment blossoms within them — a tangible reward for their hard work and dedication.

Summer Bridge Building Activities books transcend traditional educational tools; they are meticulously crafted to build a deep and enduring understanding of mathematics. These books follow a sequential and logical progression, starting from fundamental principles and advancing to sophisticated problem-solving strategies. Each chapter is designed to build on the previous one, ensuring a solid and comprehensive foundation for future learning.

Parents, we yearn for nothing more than to see our children thrive academically and personally. We want to witness the spark of inspiration ignited within them as they overcome academic challenges with confidence and poise. Summer Bridge Building Activities books serve as indispensable partners in this noble endeavor, offering not just practice questions but the keys to unlocking a world of academic and personal opportunities.

Visualize the pride on your child's face as they master a challenging math concept, the joy they experience when their efforts yield results, and the confidence they gain with each success. These pages are designed to make learning math a positive, enriching, and deeply rewarding experience that will benefit them throughout their academic journey and beyond.

For educators, Summer Bridge Building Activities books are invaluable allies in the quest to cultivate mathematical proficiency in the classroom. Accompanied by comprehensive guides and readily available answers, instructors can focus on mentoring and nurturing their students, secure in the knowledge that these books provide a robust framework for effective learning.

Within the pages of Summer Bridge Building Activities books lies not just the promise of academic excellence, but the seeds of a brighter future. By integrating these resources into your child's summer routine, you are bestowing upon them the gifts of confidence, curiosity, and a lifelong love of learning.

Invest in your child's future today with Summer Bridge Building Activities books — because every great journey begins with a single step, and this step can change everything. Keep the momentum of learning alive over the summer, and watch your child soar to new academic heights.

Contents

Grade
7 - 9
PRE ALGEBRA
WORKBOOK
BRIDGE BUILDING
ACTIVITIES
Equations, Inequalities
and Expressions
Linear Equations
Graphing and Slope
System of Equations
Quadratic Equations

Grade
6 - 8
PRE ALGEBRA
WORKBOOK
BRIDGE BUILDING
ACTIVITIES
Equations
One Side and Two Sides
Verbal Algebra
Expressions
Linear Equations and Slope
Order of Operations

Grade
5 - 6
PRE ALGEBRA
WORKBOOK
BRIDGE BUILDING
ACTIVITIES
Integers, Mixed Numbers
Decimals and Fractions
Place Value
Exponents and Roots
Percentage and Ratio
Word Problems

PRE ALGEBRA
WORKBOOK
for
Beginners
Integers
Fractions, Mixed Numbers
Place Value
Exponents and Roots
Percentage
Ratio Conversion

PRE ALGEBRA
WORKBOOK
for
Adults
Integers
Percent and Ratio
Equations, Inequalities
Expressions
Order of Operations

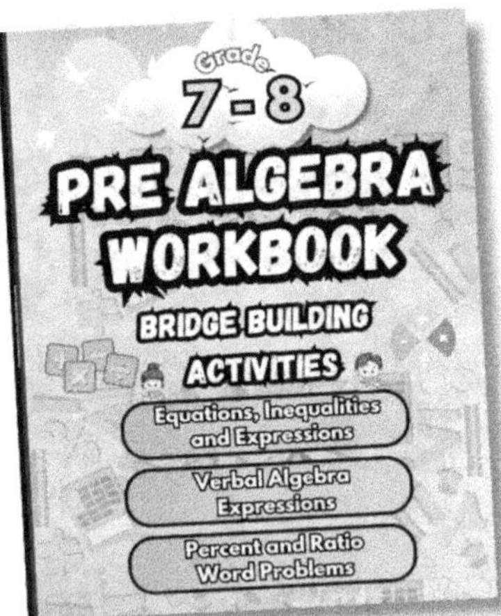

Grade
7 - 8
PRE ALGEBRA
WORKBOOK
BRIDGE BUILDING
ACTIVITIES
Equations, Inequalities
and Expressions
Verbal Algebra
Expressions
Percent and Ratio
Word Problems

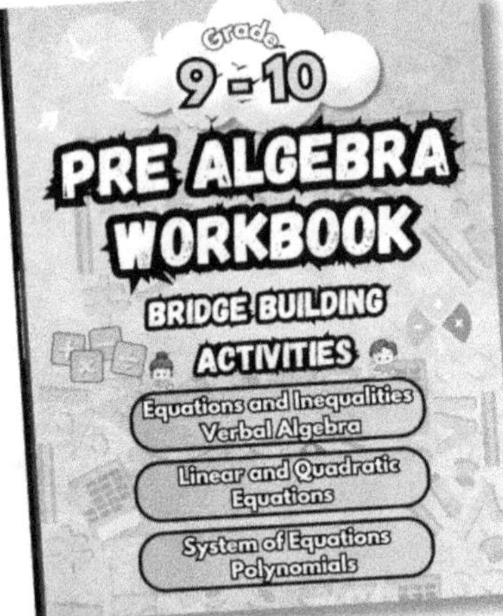

Grade
9 - 10
PRE ALGEBRA
WORKBOOK
BRIDGE BUILDING
ACTIVITIES
Equations and Inequalities
Verbal Algebra
Linear and Quadratic
Equations
System of Equations
Polynomials

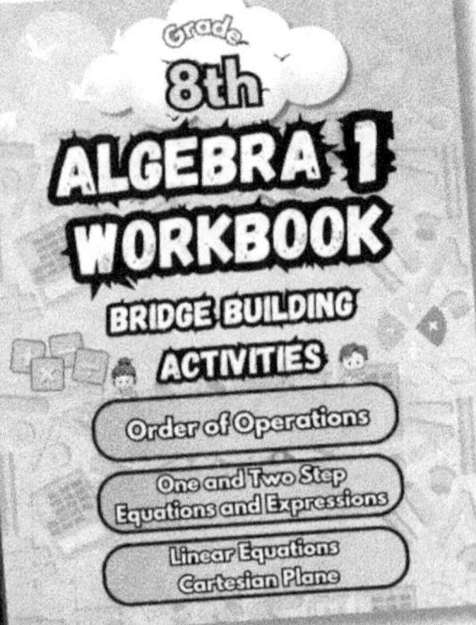

Grade
8th
ALGEBRA 1
WORKBOOK
BRIDGE BUILDING
ACTIVITIES
Order of Operations
One and Two Step
Equations and Expressions
Linear Equations
Cartesian Plane

Grade
7 - 9
ALGEBRA 1
WORKBOOK
BRIDGE BUILDING
ACTIVITIES
Integers
Order of Operations
One and Multi Step
Equations and Expressions
Linear, Quadratic Equations
Equations One Side, Two Sides

Operations with Rational Numbers

Positive and negative integers are whole numbers that can represent quantities greater than zero and less than zero, respectively.

Positive Integers: Positive integers are whole numbers greater than zero. They are denoted by the numbers 1,2,3,4...

Negative Integers: Negative integers are whole numbers less than zero. They are denoted by placing a negative sign ("-") before the numbers, such as
$-1,-2,-3,-4,...$

The positive integers are used to represent the number of objects, scores, etc. whereas the negative integers can be used to represent debt, losses, temperatures below freezing points, etc.

Let's solve some problems:

1. 6 – (– 8) – 9

- Start by simplifying within the parentheses:

$$- (-8) \text{ becomes } 8.$$

- Rewrite the expression with the simplified part:

$$6 + 8 - 9.$$

- Now perform addition and subtraction from left to right:

$$6 + 8 = 1\,4, \text{ then } 14 - 9 = 5$$

2. (– 5) – (– 3) + 10

$$(-5) + 3 + 10$$

$$(-5) + 3 = -2, \text{ then } -2 + 10 = 8$$

Rational Numbers: Operations

Evaluate Expressions.

1) $2 - 4 + 6 =$

2) $7 + 4 - 9 =$

3) $2 + 4 - 5 =$

4) $8 - (-4) - 10 =$

5) $9 + 1 - 5 =$

6) $(-2) + 2 =$

7) $6 - (-3) - 3 =$

8) $(-4) - 1 + (-1) =$

9) $(-8) + (-8) + 2 =$

10) $(-2) - 4 + (-7) =$

11) $(-1) - (-1) - (-7) =$

12) $1 - 2 + 4 =$

13) $(-1) - (-1) =$

14) $(-5) - 5 =$

15) $7 - 9 + 8 =$

16) $1 + (-9) =$

17) $(-3) + (-2) + 10 =$

18) $(-8) - (-3) =$

19) $10 + 3 - 7 =$

20) $(-3) + (-2) =$

21) $(-8) - 1 + (-3) =$

22) $9 - 10 + 2 =$

23) $(-8) + (-9) - 8 =$

24) $4 - 7 + 8 =$

25) $(-9) + (-8) =$

26) $(-7) - (-5) - (-2) =$

27) $(-7) - 2 + (-7) =$

28) $(-4) - (-7) - (-1) =$

29) $3 + (-5) - 6 =$

30) $(-3) + (-4) - 1 =$

31) $7 - 9 - 5 =$

32) $(-4) - 10 + (-5) =$

33) $(-3) + (-8) =$

34) $2 - 6 + 3 =$

35) $10 - 1 + 10 =$

36) $(-8) - (-2) =$

37) $6 - 3 + 3 =$

38) $(-1) + 9 + (-8) =$

39) $6 - 6 + 7 =$

40) $8 + (-2) =$

41) $(-1) + 1 + (-4) =$

42) $(-4) - 10 =$

43) $4 - 8 + (-1) =$

44) $6 - (-3) =$

45) $(-4) + (-10) + 3 =$

46) $5 - (-7) =$

47) $10 - 1 + (-9) =$

48) $(-8) + (-4) + 7 =$

49) $4 + (-2) =$

50) $10 - (-3) - 10 =$

51) $(-3) + (-3) + 9 =$

52) $3 + (-10) - 8 =$

53) $(-3) + (-4) + (-3) =$

54) $8 - 9 + 3 =$

55) $(-4) - (-6) + 4 =$

56) $10 - 3 + 9 =$

57) $(-2) - (-4) + 10 =$

58) $7 + (-2) - 9 =$

59) $(-5) - (-7) + 10 =$

60) $5 + (-6) + 7 =$

61) $(-9) - (-5) - (-1) =$

62) $(-10) + (-2) =$

63) $(-5) - 2 + (-4) =$

64) $3 + (-7) + 7 =$

65) $(-10) + 2 + (-10) =$

66) $(-2) - 9 + (-5) =$

67) $(-2) + 10 + (-8) =$

68) $2 - 3 + 8 =$

69) $10 + (-10) =$

70) $6 - 1 + 1 =$

71) $(-8) + (-3) + 9 =$

72) $8 + 9 - 6 =$

73) $(-9) - (-4) =$

74) $3 + 4 - 5 =$

75) $(-9) - 8 =$

76) $9 - 6 + 6 =$

77) $(-7) - (-1) + 5 =$

78) $3 + (-7) =$

Mixed Numbers: Mixed into Improper

Mixed numbers and improper fractions are two different ways to represent the same value of a fraction.

1. **Mixed Number:** A mixed number is a combination of a whole number and a proper fraction. For example, $2\frac{1}{3}$ is a mixed number, where 2 is the whole number part and $\frac{1}{3}$ is the fraction part.

2. **Improper Fraction:** An improper fraction is a fraction where the numerator is greater than or equal to the denominator. For example, $\frac{7}{3}$ is an improper fraction because 6 is greater than 3.

To convert a mixed number to an improper fraction, you multiply the whole number by the denominator of the fraction, add the numerator, and then write the result over the original denominator. For example:

$$2\frac{1}{3} = \frac{2 \times 3 + 1}{3} = \frac{7}{3}$$

To convert an improper fraction to a mixed number, we divide the numerator by the denominator. The quotient becomes the whole number part, and the remainder becomes the numerator of the fraction. For example:

$$\frac{7}{3} = 2\frac{1}{3}$$

Mixed Numbers: Addition and Subtraction

To add or subtract mixed numbers, we follow similar steps as when adding or subtracting regular fractions. For instance:

Addition:

- <u>Add the whole numbers:</u> Add the whole number parts of the mixed numbers together.
- <u>Add the fractions:</u> Add the fractions parts of the mixed numbers together.
- <u>Simplify (if needed):</u> If the fraction part of the sum is an improper fraction, simplify it by converting it to a mixed number.

Subtraction:

- <u>Subtract the whole numbers:</u> Subtract the whole number part of the second mixed number from the whole number part of the first mixed number.
- <u>Subtract the fractions:</u> Subtract the fraction part of the second mixed number from the fraction part of the first mixed number.
- <u>Simplify (if needed):</u> If the fraction part of the difference is a negative fraction, borrow from the whole number part or simplify it by converting it to a mixed number.

Mixed Numbers: Multiplication and Division

To multiply or divide mixed numbers, we follow these steps:

Multiplication:

- Convert the mixed numbers to improper fractions: Multiply the whole number by the denominator of the fraction, then add the numerator. Write the result over the original denominator.
- Multiply the fractions: Multiply the numerators together to get the new numerator and multiply the denominators together to get the new denominator.
- Simplify (if needed): If the result is an improper fraction, simplify it by converting it back to a mixed number.

Division:

- Convert the mixed numbers to improper fractions:
- Invert the divisor: Flip the second fraction (the one you're dividing by) so that the division becomes multiplication.
- Multiply the fractions: Multiply the numerators together to get the new numerator and multiply the denominators together to get the new denominator.
- Simplify (if needed): If the result is an improper fraction, simplify it by converting it back to a mixed number.

NAME: _______________

Mixed Numbers

Calculate.

1) $7\frac{2}{3} \times 2\frac{3}{6} =$ _______________

2) $8\frac{6}{10} - 7\frac{3}{4} =$ _______________

3) $1\frac{5}{9} + 1\frac{1}{2} =$ _______________

4) $2\frac{1}{7} + 6\frac{4}{5} =$ _______________

5) $9\frac{4}{6} \times 2\frac{1}{10} =$ _______________

6) $7\frac{1}{2} + 6\frac{6}{9} =$ _______________________

7) $2\frac{1}{3} \times 1\frac{5}{8} =$ _______________________

8) $2\frac{3}{4} \times 2\frac{1}{5} =$ _______________________

9) $8\frac{1}{7} - 7\frac{1}{6} =$ _______________________

10) $1\frac{1}{2} \div 4\frac{1}{5} =$ _______________________

11) $3\frac{1}{4} \div 6\frac{3}{7} =$ _______________________________

12) $9\frac{5}{9} \times 4\frac{1}{3} =$ _______________________________

13) $8\frac{6}{8} - 5\frac{8}{10} =$ _______________________________

14) $8\frac{5}{6} \times 2\frac{1}{2} =$ _______________________________

15) $1\frac{3}{10} \times 1\frac{5}{7} =$ _______________________________

16) $3\frac{5}{8} \times 9\frac{8}{9} =$ ___________________

17) $1\frac{2}{3} + 4\frac{3}{4} =$ ___________________

18) $6\frac{4}{5} \div 9\frac{3}{6} =$ ___________________

19) $6\frac{7}{9} - 2\frac{1}{2} =$ ___________________

20) $8\frac{3}{4} - 4\frac{6}{8} =$ ___________________

21) $4\frac{1}{10} \div 9\frac{2}{5} =$ _______________________

22) $4\frac{1}{3} \div 1\frac{4}{7} =$ _______________________

23) $9\frac{1}{10} - 4\frac{5}{6} =$ _______________________

24) $1\frac{2}{3} \times 3\frac{3}{9} =$ _______________________

25) $3\frac{1}{2} - 1\frac{4}{8} =$ _______________________

26) $9\frac{3}{4} - 6\frac{3}{5} =$ ______________________

27) $9\frac{7}{10} + 3\frac{2}{7} =$ ______________________

28) $8\frac{5}{7} - 4\frac{3}{9} =$ ______________________

29) $4\frac{2}{4} \times 5\frac{3}{8} =$ ______________________

30) $8\frac{1}{3} \times 3\frac{9}{10} =$ ______________________

31) $2\frac{1}{2} + 2\frac{4}{6} =$ _______________

32) $8\frac{2}{5} \times 8\frac{4}{5} =$ _______________

33) $8\frac{1}{2} - 7\frac{1}{6} =$ _______________

34) $5\frac{1}{4} + 2\frac{4}{7} =$ _______________

35) $2\frac{3}{9} \div 4\frac{1}{3} =$ _______________

Percentage

Percentage is a way of expressing a number as a fraction of 100. It is commonly used to represent proportions, rates, and comparisons. The symbol "%" is used to denote percentages.

To calculate a percentage, we multiply the given number by the appropriate fraction or decimal equivalent.

How to calculate a percentage:

Convert Percentage to Decimal: If the percentage is given as a percentage value (e.g., 25%), convert it to its decimal equivalent by dividing by 100.

$$\text{For example, 25\% as a decimal is } \frac{25}{100} = 0.25$$

Multiply: Multiply the decimal equivalent of the percentage by the given number. This gives us the portion of the number that represents the percentage.

$$100 \times 0.25 = 25\%$$

Result: The result is the calculated percentage value.

For example, to calculate 25% of 80:

Convert 25% to a decimal: 25% = 0.25.

Multiply 0.25 by 80: $0.25 \times 80 = 20$. The result is 20.

NAME: _______________

Percentage

Find the percentage of given numbers.

1) 1% of ☐ = 8

2) 4% of 700 = ☐

3) ☐ of 100 = 6

4) 60% of 900 = ☐

5) ☐ of 200 = 140

6) 5% of 900 = ☐

7) 20% of ☐ = 8

8) 8% of ☐ = 48

9) 200% of 200 = ☐

10) 40% of ☐ = 40

11) 30% of ☐ = 60

12) 7% of 900 = ☐

13) 100% of 200 = ☐

14) 90% of ☐ = 270

15) 3% of ☐ = 6

16) 35% of ☐ = 17.5

17) 80% of ☐ = 640

18) ☐ of 700 = 2100

19) 2% of 400 = ☐

20) ☐ of 500 = 50

21) 50% of 700 = ☐

22) 25% of 900 = ☐

23) 9% of ☐ = 54

24) 15% of 800 = ☐

25) 75% of ☐ = 300

26) 100% of ☐ = 100

27) 4% of 100 = ☐

28) ☐ of 200 = 100

29) 5% of ☐ = 30

30) 2% of 800 = ☐

Percent Word Problems

Percent word problems involve situations where percentages are used to calculate quantities or amounts. These problems often require converting percentages to decimals and then applying them to the given values.

For example:

Bella bought a pair of shoes for $90.00. If she paid an additional 90% for taxes, how much in total did she pay for the shoes?

- Bella bought a pair of shoes for $90.00.
- She paid an additional 90% for taxes.

Calculate 90% of $90:

Tax= 90% × 90

Tax= 0.90 × 90

Tax= $81

Add the tax amount to the original price:

Total cost= $90 + $81

Total cost= $171

Percent Word Problems

1) A person wants to make a 72% tip on a $25.00 meal. How much should the tip be?

2) A classroom has 50 students, of which 56% are girls. How many boys are in the classroom?

3) A school has 100 students. If 25% of them play tennis, how many students play tennis?

4) Mason's monthly sales of calendars was $35.00. If he earned 60% of profit, what was his profit?

5) In a class of 100 students, 2% are boys. How many are boys?

6) Adalyn bought a book for $50.00. If she paid an additional 60% for sales tax, how much in total did she pay for the book?

7) What is 8% of 75?

8) A store is having a sale where everything is 25% off. The forks originally priced at $72.00 is now on sale. How much is the new price of forks now?

9) A school has a total of 40 teachers. If 5% of them are men, how many male teachers are there?

10) A school has 28 students. If 25% of them play baseball, how many students play baseball?

11) Kennedy bought a shoes for $50.00. If she paid an additional 8% for sales tax, how much in total did she pay for the shoes?

12) In a basket of 40 trees, 90% are red trees . How many are red trees?

13) Isabella bought some shampoos for $80.00. If she paid an additional 25% for sales tax, how much in total did she pay for the shampoos?

14) In a school of 75 students, 48% of them take the bus to school. How many students take the bus?

15) A car dealership sold 75 cars last month. If the sales increased by 84% this month, how many cars did they sell this month?

16) In a survey of 65 people, 60% said they prefer cats over dogs. How many people prefer cats?

17) A store offers 25% discount on all products. If the original price of flosses was 84, what is the sales price?

18) Grayson earned $76.00 for a week's work. If he paid 25% of it in taxes how much did he pay in taxes?

19) If the number 50 is increased by 56%, what is the value of the new number?

20) A store offers a 5% discount on all items. If Hazel buys towels originally priced at $80.00, how much money did she save?

<u>**Ratio and Proportion Word Problems**</u>

We can use the concept of proportionality in solving many word problems, for example:

If a car travels 620 miles in six hours, how far can it travel in 12 hours?

Since the car travels a certain distance in a certain amount of time, we can assume that the distance traveled is directly proportional to the time taken.

Let d be the distance the car can travel in 12 hours.

We can set up a proportion:

$$\frac{\text{Distance1}}{\text{Time1}} = \frac{\text{Distance2}}{\text{Time2}}$$

Substituting the given values:

$$\frac{620 \text{ miles}}{6 \text{ hours}} = \frac{d}{12 \text{ hours}}$$

Now, let's solve for d:

$$d = \frac{620 \times 12}{6} = \frac{7440}{6} = 1240$$

So, the car can travel 1240 miles in 12 hours.

Ratio and Proportion Word Problems

1) Lincoln drives 125 miles in four hours. How far can he travel in 13 hours?

2) A bike travels at a speed of 11 miles per hour. How long will it take to travel 51 miles?

3) If it takes three students nine hours to complete a science project, how many students are needed to finish the project in 10 hours?

4) A bus travels at a speed of 62 miles per hour. How long will it take to travel 198 miles?

5) A road is 115 miles long and it takes a car three hour to travel the entire length. What is the speed of the car in miles per hour?

6) A train travels 228 miles in two hours. How far can it travel in six hours?

7) A school has a ratio of five female teachers to every 10 male teachers. If there are 27 male teachers, how many female teachers are there?

8) A rectangular pool has an area of 427 square meters and a width of 10 meters. What is the length of the pool?

9) A charity received a donation of $4,655 from a company. If the donation was divided among five charities in the ratio 2:3:4:5:6, how much did the fourth charity receive?

10) A room has an area of 185 square meters and a length of 17 meters. What is the width of the room?

11) A school has a teacher-student ratio of 1:27. If there are 965 students, how many teachers are needed?

12) A machine can produce 193 units of a product in seven hours. How long will it take to produce 375 units?

13) If a car travels 209 miles using 13 gallons of gas, how far can it travel using 16 gallons of gas?

14) A school has a ratio of five teachers for every 20 students. If the school has 108 students, how many teachers are there?

15) If a recipe calls for five eggs for every seven cups of flour, how many eggs are needed for 12 cups of flour?

16) If 10 workers can build a wall in 20 hours, how many workers are needed to build the wall in six hours?

17) A charity received a donation of $3,130 from a company. If the donation was divided among five charities in the ratio 2:3:4:5:6, how much did the third charity receive?

18) A zoo has a ratio of five monkeys to every eight lions. If there are 38 lions in the zoo, how many monkeys are there?

19) In a classroom, the ratio of boys to girls is two:nine. If there are 13 girls, how many boys are there?

20) If six workers can complete a job in 14 days, how many workers are needed to complete the job in seven days?

21) A company has a ratio of two female employees to every six male employees. If there are 30 male employees, how many female employees are there?

Order of Operations (PEMDAS)

The order of operations, often remembered by the acronym PEMDAS, stands for:

- **Parentheses**: Perform operations inside parentheses first.
- **Exponents**: Evaluate exponents (powers and roots) next.
- **Multiplication and Division**: Perform multiplication and division from left to right.
- **Addition and Subtraction:** Perform addition and subtraction from left to right.

The order of operations helps to clarify which operations should be performed first in a mathematical expression to ensure consistent and accurate results.

- **Parentheses**: Evaluate expressions within parentheses first. If there are nested parentheses, start with the innermost ones and work your way out.

    1. Example: $2 \times (3 + 4) = 2 \times 7 = 14$

- **Exponents**: Evaluate expressions with exponents (powers and roots) next.

    1. Example: $2^3 + 4 = 8 + 4 = 12$

- **Multiplication and Division**: Perform multiplication and division from left to right.

    1. Example: $2 \times 3 + 4 = 6 + 4 = 10$

    2. Example: $6 \div 2 \times 3 = 3 \times 3 = 9$

- **Addition and Subtraction**: Perform addition and subtraction from left to right.

    1. Example: $2 + 3 \times 4 = 2 + 12 = 14$

    2. Example: $10 - 4 \div 2 = 10 - 2 = 8$

Order of Operations (PEMDAS)

1) $6 + 8 + 5 =$

2) $(4 + 9)^2 + (5 + 2)^2 =$

3) $(5 + 8)^2 =$

4) $8 + 1 - 9 + 5 =$

5) $9 + 5 + 3 + 6 =$

6) $6 + 5^2 + 8 + 9^2 =$

7) $10 + 1^2 =$

8) $10 + 7^2 + 4 + 4^2 =$

9) $5 + 3^2 =$

10) $5 + 7 + 10 + 7 =$

11) $8 + 2 + 9 =$

12) $(3 + 1)(4 + 7) =$

13) $10 \times 5 \times 7 =$

14) $4 + 9 + 8 =$

15) $7 \times 1 \times 5 =$

16) $5 + 6 + 9 + 9 =$

17) $(10^2) \times (4^2) + 7 =$

18) $8 \times 6 + 7 =$

19) $(5 + 1)(8 + 3) =$

20) $3 + 2 - 2 + 3 =$

21) $8 + 7 + 7 =$

22) $(1 + 6) \div 3 =$

23) $9 \times 8 + 4 =$

24) $(3 + 8) \div 2 =$

25) $10 \times 8 \times 4 =$

26) $(10 + 8) \times (10 + 8) =$

27) $(2 + 7) \div 4 =$

28) $6 \times 2 \times 7 =$

29) $5 + 10^2 + 7 + 3^2 =$

30) $(3 \times 4) - (3 + 7) =$

31) $(5 + 10)(4 + 9) =$

32) $(4 + 10)^2 + (7 + 10)^2 =$

33) $3 \times 1 + 4 =$

34) $10 \times (5 + 7) =$

35) $8 + 8 - 8 + 5 =$

36) $4(4 + 1) =$

37) $6 + 4 - 2 + 5 =$

38) $4 \times 2 =$

Solving One-Step Equations

Solving one-step equations involves finding the value of the variable that makes the equation true. In a one-step equation, there is only one operation (addition, subtraction, multiplication, or division) performed on the variable.

The goal is to isolate the variable on one side of the equation by performing inverse operations.

For example:

Given the equation $6 = -3z$, where we want to solve for z.

The given equation is already in the form of a one-step equation, with z being multiplied by -3.

To isolate z, we need to perform the inverse operation of multiplication, which is division.

Divide both sides by -3:

$$\frac{6}{-3} = \frac{-3z}{-3}$$

Simplify:

$$-2 = z$$

So, the solution to the equation is $z = -2$.

When we substitute the value of $z = -2$ back into the original equation, $6 = -3(-2)$, it simplifies to $6 = 6$. This confirms that our solution is correct because it satisfies the original equation.

Solving One-Step Equations

Solve for the variable.

1) $7 \times b + 9 = 72$

2) $(z \div 3) + z = 13.3$

3) $7 = y + 1$

4) $8 \times (z - 10) = 0$

5) $8.8 = k + (6 \div k)$

6) $104 = 8(6 + x)$

7) $0.6 = 6 \div k$

8) $90 = 8 \times s + s$

9) $2y - 9 = 5$

10) $21 = k \times 4 - 3$

11) $9.1 = m + (1 \div m)$

12) $b \times 6 + 4 = 58$

13) $a + 5 = 7$

14) $9(3 - a) = -36$

15) $8(1 + x) = 72$

16) $13 = 6 + x$

17) $4s + s = 30$

18) $1(2 + k) = 6$

19) $18 = s \times 6$

20) $29 = 3s + 2$

21) $40 = 6 \times m + 4$

22) $(4 \div s) + 1 = 1.4$

23) $4 \times m + m = 25$

24) $42 = s + (s \times 6)$

25) $14 = b \times 9 - 4$

26) $(m \times 1) + m = 8$

27) $52 = 10 \times z + 2$

28) $20 = 2 + (2 \times b)$

29) $18 = z \times 8 + z$

30) $6.7 = (4 \div k) + 6$

31) $z \times 1 = 7$

32) $7x - x = 12$

33) $5b + 2 = 22$

34) $18 = m + m$

35) $7 \times s + s = 80$

36) $1 \times (a - 6) = -1$

37) $0.4 = x \div 10$

38) $-40 = k \times (3 - k)$

39) $1.4 = 1 + (a \div 10)$

40) $9 = (3 \times x) + 6$

41) $6m - 1 = 29$

42) $5 = k + (4 \div k)$

43) $(x \div 9) + x = 1.1$

44) $3 = (y \times 2) + y$

45) $32 = 2(9 + b)$

46) $10 = (s \div 4) + s$

47) $9 = 3(6 - m)$

48) $56 = y \times 7$

Solving Equations (One Side)

Solving one-step equations involves performing a single operation to isolate the variable and find its value.

Let's solve an equation step by step: $16 + x = 31$

1. Identify the Goal:

    The goal is to isolate the variable x on one side of the equation.

2. Simplify the Equation: Combine like terms on both sides of the equation, if necessary.

    The equation is already simplified.

3. Undo Addition or Subtraction: If there's addition or subtraction involving the variable, undo it by performing the opposite operation on both sides of the equation.

    Since x is being added to 16, we'll undo this operation by subtracting 16 from both sides of the equation:
    $$16 + x - 16 = 31 - 16$$

4. Isolate the Variable: Ensure that the variable is alone on one side of the equation.

    $$x = 15$$

5. Check Your Solution: Substitute the value of x back into the original equation to verify that it satisfies the equation.

    $$16 + 15 = 31$$

    $$31 = 31$$

The equation is balanced.

Equations: (One Side)

Solve the equations for the variable.

1) $k + 3 = 15$

2) $10 + x = 14$

3) $y \times 15 = -60$

4) $-8 \div y = -4$

5) $17 - y = 8$

6) $y + 20 = 39$

7) $-15 \div x = 3$

8) $20y + 0 = 120$

9) $8 - y = 6$

10) $-10k + 4 = -126$

11) $14 \div y = 7$

12) $0 + y = 19$

13) $8y + 10 = 82$

14) $16 + y = 35$

15) $19 + 12k = -77$

16) $13 \times k = 104$

17) $z \div -3 = 2$

18) $13 - 3y = 4$

19) $z + 9 = 4$

20) $-1 + 19m = 170$

21) $z \times 13 = -117$

22) $388 - 20x = 8$

23) $10y + -1 = 119$

24) $-10 \times m = -50$

25) $m - -3 = 3$

26) $k - -2 = 10$

27) $-16 \div k = -4$

28) $-4m + 4 = -20$

29) $-7 \times k = 21$

30) $3x - 11 = 1$

31) $z \div 2 = -10$

32) $z \times 13 = -104$

33) $m + 9 = 15$

34) $x - -10 = 22$

35) $y \div 7 = 10$

36) $y \times 6 = 0$

37) $3k - 5 = 1$

38) $1x - 14 = 2$

39) $7m - 20 = 29$

40) $m \div -8 = -7$

41) $0 + m = -2$

42) $-2 - z = 3$

43) $-9 + y = -2$

44) $20 + m = 37$

45) $16 + x = 28$

46) $m \times 15 = 15$

47) $19y - -3 = 136$

48) $3 + m = 22$

49) $-4 \times z = -4$

50) $k \div 2 = -4$

51) $y \div 11 = -6$

52) $z \div 12 = -2$

53) $14 + x = 20$

54) $k \times -4 = 40$

55) $y - -3 = 22$

56) $-1 + 11x = 43$

<u>**Evaluating Equations**</u>

Evaluating expressions involves substituting given values for variables in an expression and then performing the indicated operations to find the result.

For example: Let's evaluate $4x - 10$, when $x = 3$:

Step 1: Substitute the given value for the variable:

Replace every occurrence of x in the expression $4x - 10$ with the given value, which is 3:

$$= 4(3) - 10$$

Step 2: Perform the operations:

Perform the indicated operations according to the order of operations (PEMDAS - Parentheses, Exponents, Multiplication and Division, Addition and Subtraction):

$$= 4 \times 3 - 10$$

Step 3: Simplify:

Calculate the result:

$$12 - 10 = 2$$

Evaluating Equations

Simplify the following equations when the value of n = -8

1) (5n + 0) + (-7n – 10) =

2) -3(-10 + n) =

3) -1n + n =

4) n – 1 =

5) -8 + -9n =

6) 6 + n =

7) -1n + 5n – 10 =

8) -3n + n =

Evaluating Equations

Simplify the following equations when the value of n = -8

1) $n + 9 + 3n =$

2) $9(3 + n) =$

3) $6n + n =$

4) $10 + n =$

5) $(n + -6) \div 2 =$

6) $n + -8 + 7n =$

7) $6n - n =$

8) $-1 + \dfrac{n}{-1} =$

SUMMER ALGEBRA WORKBOOK
BUILDING ACTIVITIES

Evaluating Equations

Simplify the following equations when the value of $n = 3$

1) $\dfrac{n}{3} + \text{-}4 =$

2) $4n + 3 + (\text{-}7n - 5) =$

3) $7 \div n =$

4) $3^2 + n^2 =$

5) $0n + \text{-}10 =$

6) $\dfrac{n}{3} + \text{-}6 =$

7) $\text{-}4(0 + n) =$

8) $7n + n =$

Evaluating Equations

Simplify the following equations when the value of n = -4

1) $n(9 + n) =$

2) $-7 + \dfrac{n}{-1} =$

3) $9 + (-1n + 8) =$

4) $(6n)^2 =$

5) $-3n + 6n + 2n =$

6) $\dfrac{n}{-2} =$

7) $n^1 + n - -6 =$

8) $10n + -2 + (4n - 9) =$

SUMMER ALGEBRA WORKBOOK

BUILDING ACTIVITIES

Evaluating Equations

Simplify the following equations when the value of $n = -2$

1) $n + 9 + n =$

2) $n + \text{-}7 =$

3) $5n + n =$

4) $6 + \dfrac{n}{-2} =$

5) $\text{-}1 - n =$

6) $(\text{-}7n)^2 =$

7) $n \div 7 =$

8) $8 + (0n + 10) =$

Evaluating Equations

Simplify the following equations when the value of n = -9

1) $n - 1 =$

2) $-1n + 4n + -1n =$

3) $-6n - n =$

4) $-2n + 5n - 10 =$

5) $-5n + -8 =$

6) $(n^2 + -6) - -4(5 + n) =$

7) $\dfrac{9 + -9}{n + 8} =$

8) $n + 4 =$

Evaluating Equations

Simplify the following equations when the value of n = -7

1) $8n + -7 =$

2) $5 + n =$

3) $-7n + 4n + 10n =$

4) $8 + n =$

5) $-10n - n =$

6) $-3 \div (n + -2) =$

7) $-8 \div n + -4 =$

8) $2n + -10 =$

Evaluating Equations

Simplify the following equations when the value of $n = -3$

1) $-5n + 7n + n =$

2) $n + 8 + -7n =$

3) $4n + -2 =$

4) $n - 10 =$

5) $-5n + -3n - -5 =$

6) $10n + n =$

7) $6 + 2n =$

8) $n^1 + n - -8 =$

Evaluating Equations

Simplify the following equations when the value of n = -5

1) $\dfrac{-20}{n} =$

2) $-10n + n =$

3) $2 \div n + 1 =$

4) $0n + 10n - 4 =$

5) $-7 + n =$

6) $7n + -4 =$

7) $n + 8 + 8n =$

8) $-2 + (9n + 8) =$

ANSWERS

Page 1:   Rational Numbers: Operations

1. 4 **2.** 2 **3.** 1 **4.** 2 **5.** 5 **6.** 0 **7.** 6 **8.** -6 **9.** -14

10. -13 **11.** 7 **12.** 3 **13.** 0 **14.** -10 **15.** 6 **16.** -8 **17.** 5 **18.** -5

19. 6 **20.** -5 **21.** -12 **22.** 1 **23.** -25 **24.** 5 **25.** -17 **26.** 0 **27.** -16

28. 4 **29.** -8 **30.** -8 **31.** -7 **32.** -19 **33.** -11 **34.** -1 **35.** 19 **36.** -6

37. 6 **38.** 0 **39.** 7 **40.** 6 **41.** -4 **42.** -14 **43.** -5 **44.** 9 **45.** -11

46. 12 **47.** 0 **48.** -5 **49.** 2 **50.** 3 **51.** 3 **52.** -15 **53.** -10 **54.** 2

55. 6 **56.** 16 **57.** 12 **58.** -4 **59.** 12 **60.** 6 **61.** -3 **62.** -12 **63.** -11

64. 3 **65.** -18 **66.** -16 **67.** 0 **68.** 7 **69.** 0 **70.** 6 **71.** -2 **72.** 11

73. -5 **74.** 2 **75.** -17 **76.** 9 **77.** -1 **78.** -4

Page 9:   Mixed Numbers

1. 19 1/6 **2.** 17/20 **3.** 3 1/18 **4.** 8 33/35 **5.** 20 3/10

6. 14 1/6 **7.** 3 19/24 **8.** 6 1/20 **9.** 41/42 **10.** 5/14

11. 91/180 **12.** 41 11/27 **13.** 2 19/20 **14.** 22 1/12 **15.** 2 8/35

16. 35 61/72 **17.** 6 5/12 **18.** 68/95 **19.** 4 5/18 **20.** 4

21. 41/94 **22.** 2 25/33 **23.** 4 4/15 **24.** 5 5/9 **25.** 2

26. 3 3/20 **27.** 12 69/70 **28.** 4 8/21 **29.** 24 3/16 **30.** 32 1/2

31. 5 1/6 **32.** 73 23/25 **33.** 1 1/3 **34.** 7 23/28 **35.** 7/13

Page 16:   Percentage

1. 800 **2.** 28 **3.** 6% **4.** 540 **5.** 70% **6.** 45 **7.** 40

8. 600   **9.** 400   **10.** 100   **11.** 200   **12.** 63   **13.** 200   **14.** 300

15. 200   **16.** 50   **17.** 800   **18.** 300%   **19.** 8   **20.** 10%   **21.** 350

22. 225   **23.** 600   **24.** 120   **25.** 400   **26.** 100   **27.** 4   **28.** 50%

29. 600   **30.** 16

Page 19:   Percent Word Problems

1. $18.00   **2.** 22   **3.** 25   **4.** $21.00   **5.** 2

6. $80.00   **7.** 6   **8.** $54.00   **9.** 2   **10.** 7

11. $54.00   **12.** 36   **13.** $100.00   **14.** 36   **15.** 138

16. 39   **17.** 63   **18.** $19.00   **19.** 22   **20.** $4.00

Page 24:   Ratio and Proportion Word Problems

1. 406.25   **2.** 4.64   **3.** 2.7   **4.** 3.19   **5.** 38.33   **6.** 684

7. 13.5   **8.** 42.7   **9.** 1,163.75   **10.** 10.88   **11.** 35.74   **12.** 13.60

13. 257.23   **14.** 27   **15.** 8.57   **16.** 33.33   **17.** 626   **18.** 23.75

19. 2.89   **20.** 12   **21.** 10

Page 31:   Order of Operations (PEMDAS)

1. 19   **2.** 218   **3.** 169   **4.** 5   **5.** 23   **6.** 120   **7.** 11

8. 79   **9.** 14   **10.** 29   **11.** 19   **12.** 44   **13.** 350   **14.** 21

15. 35   **16.** 29   **17.** 1,607   **18.** 55   **19.** 66   **20.** 6   **21.** 22

22. 2.3   **23.** 76   **24.** 5.5   **25.** 320   **26.** 324   **27.** 2.2   **28.** 84

29. 121   **30.** 2   **31.** 195   **32.** 485   **33.** 7   **34.** 120   **35.** 13

36. 20   **37.** 13   **38.** 8

Page 35:   Solving One-Step Equations

1. 9	**2.** 10	**3.** 6	**4.** 10	**5.** 8	**6.** 7
7. 10	**8.** 10	**9.** 7	**10.** 6	**11.** 9	**12.** 9
13. 2	**14.** 7	**15.** 8	**16.** 7	**17.** 6	**18.** 4
19. 3	**20.** 9	**21.** 6	**22.** 9	**23.** 5	**24.** 6
25. 2	**26.** 4	**27.** 5	**28.** 9	**29.** 2	**30.** 6
31. 7	**32.** 2	**33.** 4	**34.** 9	**35.** 10	**36.** 5
37. 4	**38.** 8 or -5	**39.** 4	**40.** 1	**41.** 5	**42.** 4 or 1
43. 1	**44.** 1	**45.** 7	**46.** 8	**47.** 3	**48.** 8

Page 41:   Equations: (One Side)

1. $k = 12$	**2.** $x = 4$	**3.** $y = -4$	**4.** $y = 2$	**5.** $y = 9$	**6.** $y = 19$
7. $x = -5$	**8.** $y = 6$	**9.** $y = 2$	**10.** $k = 13$	**11.** $y = 2$	**12.** $y = 19$
13. $y = 9$	**14.** $y = 19$	**15.** $k = -8$	**16.** $k = 8$	**17.** $z = -6$	**18.** $y = 3$
19. $z = -5$	**20.** $m = 9$	**21.** $z = -9$	**22.** $x = 19$	**23.** $y = 12$	**24.** $m = 5$
25. $m = 0$	**26.** $k = 8$	**27.** $k = 4$	**28.** $m = 6$	**29.** $k = -3$	**30.** $x = 4$
31. $z = -20$	**32.** $z = -8$	**33.** $m = 6$	**34.** $x = 12$	**35.** $y = 70$	**36.** $y = 0$
37. $k = 2$	**38.** $x = 16$	**39.** $m = 7$	**40.** $m = 56$	**41.** $m = -2$	**42.** $z = -5$
43. $y = 7$	**44.** $m = 17$	**45.** $x = 12$	**46.** $m = 1$	**47.** $y = 7$	**48.** $m = 19$
49. $z = 1$	**50.** $k = -8$	**51.** $y = -66$	**52.** $z = -24$	**53.** $x = 6$	**54.** $k = -10$
55. $y = 19$	**56.** $x = 4$				

Page 48:   Evaluating Equations

1. 6	**2.** 54	**3.** 0	**4.** -9	**5.** 64	**6.** -2	**7.** -42	**8.** 16

Page 49:   Evaluating Equations

1. -23   **2.** -45   **3.** -56   **4.** 2   **5.** -7   **6.** -72   **7.** -40   **8.** 7

Page 50:   Evaluating Equations

1. -3   **2.** -11   **3.** 2.3   **4.** 18   **5.** -10   **6.** -5   **7.** -12   **8.** 24

Page 51:   Evaluating Equations

1. -20   **2.** -3   **3.** 21   **4.** 576   **5.** -20   **6.** 2   **7.** -2   **8.** -67

Page 52:   Evaluating Equations

1. 5   **2.** -9   **3.** -12   **4.** 7   **5.** 1   **6.** 196   **7.** -0.3   **8.** 18

Page 53:   Evaluating Equations

1. -10   **2.** -18   **3.** 63   **4.** -37   **5.** 37   **6.** 59   **7.** 0   **8.** -5

Page 54:   Evaluating Equations

1. -63   **2.** -2   **3.** -49   **4.** 1   **5.** 77   **6.** 0.3   **7.** -2.9   **8.** -24

Page 55:   Evaluating Equations

1. -9   **2.** 26   **3.** -14   **4.** -13   **5.** 29   **6.** -33   **7.** 0   **8.** 2

Page 56:   Evaluating Equations

1. 4   **2.** 45   **3.** 0.6   **4.** -54   **5.** -12   **6.** -39   **7.** -37   **8.** -39